One Teen's Guide to Kicking Video Game Addiction

Forward

I'm Tomer Shaked, and this book was written to highlight how I kicked my gaming addiction, and to hopefully help you as well. Video games can, inarguably, provide a fun and interactive experience when used in moderation; but 'moderation' and 'video games' aren't usually synonymous. Anyone who has ever played a video game — regardless of addiction — can attest to the fact that time simply gets lost.

Video games create the illusion of a fantasy world right from the comfort of your couch, however it's a fantasy that deprives the player of any genuine emotion. Simply put, video games create a disconnect from reality and it's that disconnect that becomes an addiction. My goal for this book is to highlight important topics associated with gaming addiction that can speak to both teens and their parents who are experiencing this conflict in their own lives. I also touch on my own experience with this addiction and how I "cut the cord" on gaming for good.

My addiction to gaming consumed a large part of my childhood. I can't get those years back. Video games deprived me of many irreplaceable experiences and moments such as time with family and friends. My wish is to help you avoid the mistakes I've made, so that you won't have to miss out on what's important in your own life–the human experience. I also hope that in reading about my journey, you will find something in this book that will help you, too, "cut the cord" for good and say goodbye to gaming.

Alright; let's get to it!

Chapter 1: The Start

I started gaming at a young age. Over the course of my addiction, my parents invested a considerable amount of money buying, and I invested a considerable amount of time, playing video games. In retrospect, two of the most valuable "commodities" on this earth–time and money–were wasted. At the time, *THE* console to own was an Xbox 360, so I'm not THAT old.

At first, despite owning the coveted Xbox 360, I didn't even play that much; school and homework came first, and my parents believed this was merely a hobby, nothing to worry about with a kid my age. After all, my classmates were gaming too, right?

By the time I turned ten, there was only time to play on the weekend, and I wasn't playing much on school days if I even had permission to play at all. Back then, I was still listening to my parents. Later, I would learn to skirt their rules to get a "fix" of gaming. At ten, I didn't feel the compulsion that was slowly, silently creeping its way into my subconscious. At that time, I wouldn't have been able to tell you what *addiction* was if you asked! I mean, is there any ten-year-old kid that knows what addiction is?

At this time, gaming hadn't taken much time away yet, nor was it a distraction worth addressing for my parents. I believe, if my video gaming had become out of control when I was ten, my parents would've put a stop to it immediately.

However, my game library slowly expanded, as did the time I spent carefully selecting titles to play. With more options, so grew the hours I spent posted up in front of a screen, losing more and more time I could've been out enjoying childhood. I became obsessed with games such as *Transformers* and the *Lego* series; I began playing these games for hours a day without realizing what was happening to my brain. That is how addiction starts.

Gaming wasn't just *one* activity I enjoyed; it had started to become the *only* activity I enjoyed. Nothing else was fun anymore. Nothing compared to playing my games. Before I discovered Xbox360, I enjoyed other technology and toys. While most of my classmates had begun to take on multiple hobbies and activities: sports, music, academics, and hanging out with friends. Gaming had become the only thing I wanted to do from the time I woke up, until I went to sleep. That's when, unbeknownst to my parents or myself, it had already become a full-blown addiction. Video games had quietly taken over my whole life, it was just impossible to see it yet.

To my parents' credit, they intervened quickly once it was clear I was spending too much time on my games. Their thoughtful, conservative intervention was to cut my game time to one hour a day, a policy that was not easy to enforce when both parents work full time.

An hour a day was reasonable game time. My parents weren't drill sergeants, (OK, I won't lie, my mom is a former drill sergeant), and they didn't simply lock up my games so I couldn't use them at all. They took the reasonable approach most parents of school-age kids would take of limiting screen time.

After all, it was known that all kids play video games *sometimes*.

My parents allowing me to still access my games for an hour a day worked for a short period of time; I didn't feel deprived of my beloved games, but I also didn't spend all my time focused on gaming; it wasn't easy to be separated from my games, but I was able to do it. That doesn't mean I wasn't thinking about the next time I would be able to game constantly, but I wasn't yet trying to get out of my responsibilities to game. Back then, I was still able to focus on more important things like my education and cultivating my relationships with family and friends. Or at least I thought that's what I was doing.

With video games constantly on my mind, cultivating relationships began to feel more like creating more excuses to avoid spending too much time out of my game room. At some point, I had enough excuses to fill a library. It's hard to pinpoint when daydreaming about my games became craving them every second of the day, but that's what happened. That's why I want to warn other kids and their parents about how insidious this problem truly is.

The more I played, the more I craved to keep playing, (craving is large part of any addiction[1]) and used every dollar of my monthly allowance on new consoles and expanding my library of games.

At some point, however, I found myself playing for countless hours when my parents weren't home. Instead of engaging in another activity, like a sport or calling a friend, I would use the free time

---

[1] ScienceDaily. (2017, May 3). *Neuroscientists seek brain basis of craving in addiction and binge eating.* ScienceDaily. Retrieved June 2, 2022, from https://www.sciencedaily.com/releases/2017/05/17050315191 5.htm

to sneak in the gaming time I was now desperately craving. I would lose track of time and quickly check in with my parents to see when they'd be home.

What I also realize now, was that at the time, I only wanted to be with friends who were as interested in and as consumed by gaming as I was. Those friends were on my invite list.

Even consequences for my actions, such as getting caught and grounded for weeks, didn't change the fact all I wanted to do was game. I began to feel resentment toward my parents for taking my games away when they felt that I was not engaged enough with the family. I thought they were annoying, and the once reasonablc policy had become something I hated. The only time I'd "like" my parents again was when my games were returned. This is true addict behavior: they gave me what I wanted, and I was nice to them. It put strain between us and damaged our relationship more than I realized at twelve. I would have to work to fix this damage years later, but first I would have to kick my gaming habit.

When I wanted to game, I would always find a way. I even enlisted the help of my older sister; I'd make deals with her to keep my gaming a secret, roping her into lying to our parents on my behalf. Much like those addicted to drugs I started to adopt the addict behavior of hiding things from my parents in fear they'd reduce my game time. I hid invitations from friends and lied about being asked to hang out, so my parents wouldn't force me to attend any parties or events. While hiding things from parents is typical teen behavior, the extent to which I was doing it was not.

I never lied to or hid anything from my parents, other than the amount of time I was playing video games. Lying is unacceptable in my household. My sister and I were raised to tell the truth, the whole truth, and nothing but the truth (so help us God), no matter what the situation. So, I did feel bad, but I just couldn't stop.

I know it's wrong, lying to your parents, wishing they weren't even home just so you can sit in front of a screen, but that's what gaming does to your personality. It isolates you from the most important parts of life. You start making poor decisions, you start to crave isolation and lose pleasure in all things, except the game itself. Winning digital gifts and prizes becomes prioritized over the most important gift of all: the gift of life.

Looking back now, free of video games, I am certain that by age ten, I had become a <u>video game addict.</u>

Chapter 2: The Idea of Gaming Addictions: How Companies Get You Addicted: "The Boring Chapter"

Everyone is familiar with the concept of addiction. But not everyone is familiar with the primary source of addiction. The primary source of addiction comes from **dopamine.** I have done my research and will provide helpful resources with the information at the back of the book.

What is dopamine? Dopamine is a neurotransmitter; produced by the adrenal gland. It also occurs in the substantia nigra of the brain. Dopamine is produced during the receipt of pleasure or reward. Illegal drugs such as cocaine and heroin produce dopamine; cigarettes are a legal means of obtaining a dopamine rush, though the health consequences of smoking are severe. Cigarettes contain nicotine, a known addictive substance that produces the same dopamine rush as its illegal counterparts. Nicotine is what gives cigarettes their addictive quality. After smoking a handful of times, one becomes hooked through the release of dopamine, and eventually, it becomes a "pack a day or more" habit, leaving the smoker unable to quit easily. The same path to addiction can be applied to video games, texting, and social media.

Screen time provides a dopamine "hit". Every like, every comment, releases a rush of good feelings deep in the brain, leaving us needing more and more to get the same feeling. Pretty soon, no number of likes, comments, or screen time is enough to fulfill that craving.

For example, when someone texts you, "Hi, how are you doing today?" the message makes you feel good, resulting in dopamine release. The dopamine rush from receiving a text is linked to how wonderful it feels to receive the instant feedback texting provides. Another example would be receiving a compliment on a social media post (a friend telling you your outfit is "fire" gives you a high).

Dopamine is released upon receiving more likes and more comments. Eventually, receiving one comment or one like per day won't be enough; at some point you'll require hundreds or thousands to get the feeling you once received from a single comment. In the end, a person becomes addicted not to the social media itself, but to how it makes them feel when they receive feedback; to the point that even negative feedback begins to feed our addiction.

So, how does dopamine relate to video game use? Video games are a scientifically proven source[2] of addiction due to their ability to "hijack" the brain's reward system. When a game reward is presented, whether it's receiving a long-coveted weapon, advancing to a new level, or purchasing coins or other "add-ons", dopamine is released. Here's the scary

---

[2] *New study identifies the most definitive signs of "Tiktok addiction"*. PsyPost. (2022, May 3). Retrieved June 2, 2022, from https://www.psypost.org/2022/05/new-study-identifies-the-most-definitive-signs-of-tiktok-addiction-63071

thing about video games: developers use this method of hijacking the brain's reward system to hook and trap children and young adults who play their games.

The flood of constant dopamine (which causes the need to play more to receive higher and higher rewards) is a win-win for content creators: kids and teens come back for more and the company makes money. The developers create this game trap, "forcing" you to come back for more and more, to maintain even a baseline of dopamine. However, attempting to maintain a baseline of dopamine is chasing something you will never get. As once addiction sets in, the brain has already been hijacked.

It isn't just video game companies that use this hijack method to lure users into addiction, subconsciously forcing them to come back for more. Nearly every company that sells a consumable product like cigarettes (for Gen Z, it's vaping), phone apps, and even television does this–but they learned and perfected the method from video game companies. While social media companies aren't selling a tangible product, they're some of the worst offenders of this scam. They rely on the phones being constantly in our hands to sell us the addiction of likes and comments.

Companies worldwide have used this addiction to hook users on whatever they're selling directly from their phones.

Ultimately, this leads to only one place: waste of time, money and most importantly, the mental and physical health of the user who was blindsided and never saw it coming.

Second only to video games, social media has become the most addictive non-tangible form of achieving a dopamine hit. Did you know teens can get high off social media? Most teenagers in 2022 have at least two forms of social media and are active on at least one of them on regular basis. Whether it's to converse with the rest of the world, read the news, or look at memes–we all use these platforms daily. These platforms include Discord, Twitter, Facebook, Instagram, Snapchat, and most recently, TikTok. Scientists[3] have recently connected TikTok specifically to different forms of addiction in teens.

According to doctors and researchers in the field of addiction, any social media can harm the developing brains of kids and teens to such an extent that intervention may be required. Many parents are unfamiliar with the apps teens are using these days, as it's becoming more and more uncommon to use parental controls to restrict adolescents' access to content on the web. These apps, specifically TikTok, are designed to hold the attention spans of bored teens by providing constant content at

---

[3] *New study identifies the most definitive signs of "Tiktok addiction"*. PsyPost. (2022, May 3). Retrieved June 2, 2022, from https://www.psypost.org/2022/05/new-study-identifies-the-most-definitive-signs-of-tiktok-addiction-63071

unprecedented speeds. Whether it's a new "TikTok challenge" of the week or a funny dance routine, the app is designed to keep kids and teens coming back to consume more of the content.

"TikTok clips are designed to continue to engage attention and to turn away is very difficult because it's like, after you've been -- say -- fasting for three days, then there's a sumptuous meal in front of you, it's hard for anybody to pull back," said Dr. Michael Manos of Cleveland Clinic Children's Hospital.

These applications target the user's need for a dopamine hit to keep them coming back. When someone likes your Instagram or Facebook post or leaves a comment as simple as "nice photo", there's a dopamine hit. You feel good because your brain has been trained by receiving repeated rewards for returning to the app. However, apps like TikTok and Instagram can pose physical hazards to teens when the challenges become dangerous (remember "The Keke Challenge"?)

Aside from the mental health hazards, these same scientific principles apply to the addiction of video gaming and in fact, they've been studied much longer and have much scarier outcomes with much deeper research into the minds of those who have become addicted to them.

Sometimes we produce dopamine, and we aren't even aware of it. For example, when playing a video game, the brain constantly produces dopamine. It's a constant bombardment of rewards all at once. An excellent example of this is *Fortnite Battle Royale*. *Fortnite* is a hundred player vs. player battle royale game: the last one standing out of a hundred wins. Dopamine is produced upon winning a match, eliminating an opponent, acquiring a powerful weapon, or getting lucky. These are just a handful of prime examples of ways dopamine is produced while playing a single video game. Scientists have begun to research the effects *Fortnite* specifically has on the brains of teenagers, due to extreme addiction to the game, which is becoming more prevalent than ever.

These apps, social media platforms, and video games all hijack the dopamine-producing system. As you continuously use these applications to receive the dopamine hit, the receptors dull with time, making it harder and eventually impossible to produce dopamine at all.

Can you imagine a life where you could never feel joy again because you wasted all the dopamine you'll ever have on *video games*? That is why many teens play video games for increasingly longer periods of time in a single session. They're looking for a way to receive that rush of dopamine again, but they've become unable to feel it. Ultimately, one hour turns into multiple hours or days spent in a dark room, craving a dopamine rush just out of reach, and not understanding why you can't achieve it like you once did.

Addiction brings other "friends" to the "party" with it: depression, isolation, loneliness, boredom, and reclusiveness.

For many, this may be the first time hearing a scientific explanation of the science of addiction behavior, specifically where it relates to gaming. I didn't even know this was a real thing until I stopped gaming! The lack of dopamine eventually caught up to me, and I started to sacrifice a lot more than anyone could imagine for my next hit.

There are thousands of games out there with the same effect on the brain and there's no telling which game will get teens hooked and which won't. This is one way I began to understand why I needed to quit cold turkey and never look back.

Chapter 3: The Development

Back to me.

By age 12, I was up to my neck in gaming; it consumed every free waking moment; it was the only thing I thought about and it had begun to eat away at my life, as well as took away all my free time. I began to develop bad habits (constantly lying to my parents about how much time I spent on the game, what time I went to sleep, and let them think I wasn't spending as much time gaming as I was). The lying, assumptions, and constant gaming had started to erode the relationship I had with my parents. I am the son of two lawyers who raised me better than the pre-teen I was becoming, and yet I didn't care. I could remember a time when I did care, but it had long passed, and now all I wanted to do was game, game, game.

Looking back there *was* a catalyst for why I found myself addicted to gaming at such a young age. I experienced loss. Before the addiction fully took hold of me, I was a swimmer. From the time I was child, I'd devoted my life to swimming at the highest level I could achieve. My parents and I flew to Los Angeles to train with prestigious coaches that could help me build a career as a swimmer. I was lucky enough to meet Michael Phelps at Florida International University, where I was a team member at the time. He was training for the Beijing Olympics; I was training to be the next Michael Phelps.

But then "it" happened. "It" was the end of my swimming career before it had even jumped off, so to speak. I was eleven, but I remember it like it was yesterday.

I was practicing diving while my friend was in the water. As I dove and swam to the bottom of the pool, my friend accidentally kicked me in my left ear. Within minutes, I experienced pain like never before. It felt as if a gallon of water was inside my ear. The kick was so forceful that I learned later it had completely shattered my eardrum.

Eventually, I underwent reconstructive surgery of the ear, and spent months in recovery.

After consulting with several experts, my parents informed me that swimming was no longer an option for me. Being on a swim team and practicing every single day was a big part of my life; with that gone, I now had even more time to spend in front of my computer screen.

Eventually I joined the high school crew team in 9th grade, an activity that allowed me to be near the water, what I loved most. However, school shut down in the middle of 9th grade due to COVID, I didn't return to practice until the end of 10th grade.

Michael Phelps and Me, Tomer!

I grieved the loss of my favorite sport, and possibly a bright future as a competitive swimmer, but taking on crew– a new sport which I love just as much– allowed me to move forward. I don't look back with anger or sadness.

This experience taught me that when one door closes, another opens. I believe this knowledge and experience allowed me to have the courage to quit my video gaming addiction, while never looking back with regret. I believe any teen that has the desire to quit video games for good, can do it. I know that if I could do it, so could you. The addictive behavior is all in our heads.

At 12, I didn't understand that what I thought was *fun* was hurting me in more ways than I could ever imagine. I had no idea what I was throwing away just to sit in front of a screen in a dark room all day long. Though, I eventually found out the hard way... (I told you this story gets much worse before it gets better).

The second I came home from school all my parents' restrictions on gaming went out the window and did so for the next seven years, around the same time I had my "snap". Rules? What were those? They no longer applied to me. I played for hours regardless of their wishes. They wanted what was best for me: to study, spend time outside or with my friends, and to not constantly feel the need to run back to my games. I didn't realize how much time I was losing or how much money I was wasting, and my parents didn't always stop me.

The amount of lying I was doing to be able to play my games was substantial to the point of fooling everyone around me. That's how addicted I'd become: I was able to convince my parents, who were always on top of my academics and activities, never letting things slip past them, that I wasn't throwing my life away on gaming, and that I was getting everything else done first.

Once I realized my parents may have forgotten about the restriction, the one they had set for me when I was 10, I took advantage of it. I would play for hours, ultimately disconnecting myself from reality.

As time went on, I poured more time and energy into *Minecraft* and *Call of Duty*. I was enjoying my disconnect from reality. I didn't have to spend time in the real world where peer pressure and teachers caused me stress and anxiety. Losing myself in video games became an escape for me instead of a relaxing reward once in a while.

At this point, I didn't understand that this "escape" didn't make any sense. What was I really trying to escape from? I have a great life, great parents, and a great sister and friends. My parents provided for me and worked hard to give me experiences for which I am grateful and appreciative. We traveled, spent time together, and gained an understanding of life that would hopefully serve me well as an adult. Addiction had taken over my life and made me think it was the only thing that would make me happy and fulfilled.

After I kicked my addiction, I began to spend time reflecting on this period in my life. Looking back now, I sometimes burst into laughter when I think about how ridiculous I'd become. I can remember when being on vacation felt like jail time.

On Xbox, the "friends" I spoke to weren't real. I would call them my friends, but I didn't bother to keep in touch with those I met through the internet.

After a few months, I started pouring so much time into gaming that I neglected my academics. I would start to fail (in my house, that meant Bs instead of my regular straight As). This was because in many of my classes, I didn't devote the time needed to truly succeed. My parents noticed this and told me that if they didn't see the return of the straight As, I would lose my gaming privileges **forever**. I complied, put more time into studying, and eventually the straight As returned. However, once my grades bounced back, I would return to playing Xbox for a few months, losing more and more time than I was aware of, the cycle repeating itself.

For my 13th birthday, I received something that turned my minor addiction to gaming into a major addiction: a gaming laptop. I'd wanted one since I was in third grade, and eventually, my parents gifted me my most prized possession. After the gift of my gaming laptop, I spent even *more time* gaming than before. Was that even possible? Unfortunately, it was.

With the gaming computer, I communicated with friends using Discord and Skype, but I was so deep in my addiction I only used these apps to find other teens who wanted to game. I would contact these virtual friends online, and we'd play *Minecraft* and *Fortnite* for hours. Eventually, I stopped participating in social events, family gatherings, holidays, and vacations, and only interacted with the teens online that I had begun to use as replacements for the real-life people around me.

Do you still think video games are harmless? Maybe the next chapter of my story will finally change your mind...

Chapter 4: Consequences of Gaming

Most adults will tell you that gaming is a waste of time. Adults who offer you this advice aren't lying to you; they can see the consequences because they've either experienced them or were smart enough to stay away from video games altogether when they were our age. You're wasting your time, your money, and most importantly your life when you invest in gaming.

Picture this: your parents give you an allowance every month with little restriction on what you can do with it–so long as it's legal!

Now imagine throwing that money into the toilet or lighting it on fire! That's exactly what you do when you purchase video games or gaming consoles.

I'd guess 0.001% of teens who play video games grow up to be adults who become the next YouTube or Twitch (a gaming platform) star. The truth is, that's not likely to happen for you, and you shouldn't waste your life in front of a screen thinking it will. We all have so many other talents, skills, and intelligence we can use to better our lives and achieve greatness. All you must do is put down the game controller and walk outside. I know, I know, it's not that simple. If you're reading my story of addiction, you're potentially experiencing the same issues, or are the parent of a teen potentially experiencing the same problem.

You may have read somewhere that gaming has positives, right? Like bettering your memory and, in some cases, improving your ability to communicate. This may be true when the games are educational or challenging, but regardless, the negatives outweigh every potential positive. The negatives cause long term effects that reverberate for the rest of your life.

Let me give you a better idea of some of what happens in the throes of a gaming addiction.

Loss of Interest in Activities: Due to the vast number of games readily available at our fingertips, a person can find themselves spending hours playing a multitude of games and never feeling "bored". However, it reaches a point that someone gets so consumed with the options available to them they lose interest in anything else: sports, friends, hobbies, family, their personal health, and hygiene. It starts as a person playing a video game for a short time after school. As time goes on, he or she becomes more consumed with the game and starts to skip sports practice after school to keep playing. "I'll just skip this one practice" can turn into quitting a once-loved sport. **You won't just lose interest in sports; at that point, you've lost interest in everything.** Gaming makes most teenagers not want to go outside, hang out with their friends, go to an event, or even travel because they desire to just game.

Gaming consumes a person's identity and deprives them of critical activities.

Sedentary Living: The dictionary definition of "sedentary" is: 'tending to spend much time seated; somewhat inactive.'

Sitting or lying down for long periods of time is unhealthy. Exercise throughout the day is important for blood flow, prevention of diseases such as diabetes and heart disease. Exercising and moving our bodies is also necessary for our mental health. Exercise is scientifically proven to reduce depression and anxiety because it also produces dopamine and oxytocin (the happy hormones!) The healthiest way to achieve a dopamine or oxytocin hit is to exercise, move your body, and get outdoors. The opposite is true of gaming. It promotes sitting or lying down either on a chair or couch, which is the worst way to achieve a dopamine hit.

Gaming creates a passive form of living (you're watching life pass you by while focused only on a screen, with fake friends, living a fake life disconnected from reality). This ultimately leads to a deterioration of your health. This is especially true once a person goes from playing an hour a day or a couple of times a week to doing nothing else except gaming.

I'm starting to sound like my parents...for real!

Another example of how detrimental to physical and mental health gaming can be is when you consider someone who works 40 hours a week in an office setting. This person works as a software developer, sitting for eight hours a day, rarely getting up unless they use the bathroom or grab something to eat; things addicted gamers often don't remember to do, contributing to poor physical health very quickly. After work, he goes home and sits down on the couch, skips dinner, and just games until it's time for bed (if he even goes to sleep).

This adds up to more than 12 hours a day of screen time and sedentary habits. The person in this example can wave to their health as it walks out the door without him (because he sits all day!)

Surprisingly, most Americans with these types of jobs spend their days like this. They don't take the time to move around during the workday and are directly affected by the outcome of the examples I just described. We–children and teens–are also affected, especially in school. There is little to no movement for us anymore. Quick walks between classes offset negatively by the not-so-healthy food served during lunch. After a long day of sitting at school or at the office, we all go home and sit some more in front of their video games or tv.

Sedentary living is a long-term consequence of gaming with the health hazards recognizable almost right away. So, get up, get off the couch, and throw the controllers in the trash instead of your money!

Waste of Time: Like any addiction, **gaming is a waste of time.** I mentioned potential "positives" such as memory and communication previously, but it's not enough to justify gaming. There are a multitude of other hobbies, sports, and activities to participate in that can strengthen the mind and stretch our intelligence, helping us learn to communicate and understand the world effectively. You can acquire positive influence by surrounding yourself with family and friends. You don't need a video game for that!

Remember, exercise and fresh air can provide the same dopamine hit, safely, with **no** consequences to mental health except complete net **positives**: happiness, better physical health, and time spent with friends who care about you. Hours poured into gaming not only wastes time, but potential opportunities to better our lives.

Waste of Money: Did you know the average gamer spends $58,000 over the course of their life on games and gaming?[4] What can you do with a video game besides sit in front of a screen? Imagine what else you could do with that money!

---

[4] Murray, S. (2022, April 25). *Survey finds the average gamer spends $58,000 on gaming in their life*. TheGamer. Retrieved June 2, 2022, from https://www.thegamer.com/average-gamer-survey-spends-58000-lifetime/#:~:text=Anyway%2C%20the%20results%20of%20the,course%20of%20their%20entire%20life.

I'm embarrassed to admit this, so keep it between us, but the reality is I spent over $12,000 during the most intense four years of my gaming addiction. That's enough to invest in college tuition or buy a teenager their first car.

Speaking of cars... I was so deep into my video game addiction that when I did receive a car, that symbol of freedom for all 16-year-olds, I didn't even appreciate my gift! My parents worked hard to provide me with a car, and I couldn't have cared less about it. This hurt my dad and made him feel unappreciated. During the pandemic it was difficult to have a great birthday, but my dad went above and beyond to make my 16th as special as possible. I didn't show him the appreciation he deserved back then, because I was too involved in gaming to care about the time and money spent on me. All I knew was that having a car meant I would have to leave the house and drive it. No way! I didn't want to be away from my video games that long.

False Sense of Reality: Video games create a falsified experience that disconnects you from the world. Mom yelling for you to eat dinner with the family, or do your household chores that were supposed to be completed hours or days ago? You won't hear her! It's as if all senses are cut off completely while in the depths of a video game addiction. There is a myth that video games help you understand the world better.

Don't fall for it.

There is nothing a video game can teach you that time spent in the real world cannot. Life experiences such as traveling or being involved in a high-level sport can teach us so much more about the world than any fake reality ever could. Effective communication comes from spending time in social settings with other humans, not in front of a screen where fake people do fake things all day long. Gaming creates a false sense of reality causing a state of derealization, thus creating misinterpretation of everything around us.

It's a well-established claim that human interaction is essential to our existence. We cannot advance if we don't interact and communicate with our fellow humans. Therefore, we must not isolate ourselves behind a screen.

Isolation: Online communication is not a form of effective communication; it's not socializing. It's impossible to socialize while staring at a screen. The communication that takes place while gaming is the result of two addicted individuals engaging in that addictive behavior. Individuals communicating using a video game platform are feeding each other's addiction, and thus not socializing as one would in a social setting such as parks and sporting events.

When communicating with someone in person, you are socializing. Two people are physically present and engaging in a social interaction that allows for the sharing of emotions, feelings, and common interests. Spending all day in front of a video game or on social media is not considered socializing; there is no way to foster real friendships over the internet.

Most teens don't understand the concept that not any form of communication is socializing. They're convinced that anyone they converse with online is equally as beneficial as spending time with friends in person. This is demonstrably false.

While in the throes of a gaming addiction you become isolated from the people and places that nurture important memories and relationships. Gamers with an addiction can become defensive and hostile, claiming they're socializing because they have "online friends". That's the addiction talking. Isolating oneself, whether it's due to a video game addiction or some other unspoken issue, is harmful to our mental health. It changes a person's entire personality, strips them of who they once were, and turns them into someone they don't recognize.

Physical Pain: A sedentary lifestyle can cause constant strain on muscles, tendons, and joints. Because gaming is an activity that doesn't promote regular physical activity or body movement, it allows for loss of muscle tone, resulting in muscle weakness. Ultimately, it can lead to conditions such as arthritis and migraines.

Repetitive use of a keyboard, controller, and mouse creates what's called Carpal Tunnel Syndrome (in the 90s it was called "Nintendo thumb" or "Nintendo wrist" depending on what part of the body was injured). Carpal Tunnel Syndrome is caused by pressure on the median nerve. The carpal tunnel is a narrow passageway surrounded by bones and ligaments on the palm side of the hand. When the median nerve is compressed, symptoms can include numbness, tingling, and weakness in the hand and arm. Overuse of such things as gaming controllers, mouse, keyboard, and trackpads cause inflammation (swelling and tenderness of any area of the body; in this case the fingers, hands, and wrists), followed by compression of the median nerve. Once this happens, it could be months or years before full function is restored. That is, if it can be restored at all. Sometimes Carpal Tunnel Syndrome becomes permanent if the cause is not addressed quickly.

This isn't even an exhaustive list of consequences that can take a toll on your mental and physical health with a gaming addiction. In most cases, if time limits aren't placed on gaming and strictly adhered to it's almost guaranteed that an addiction will develop in a matter of months, if not sooner. Research now shows that games like *Fortnite* can hook an individual in a matter of *days*.[5]

---

[5] Michel Kana, P. D. (2021, November 2). *Why fortnite became the most addicting game in history*. Medium. Retrieved June 2, 2022, from https://towardsdatascience.com/why-fortnite-

Really, just throw your consoles out right now. It's not worth the risk.

I would know, all the negatives listed in this book were things I personally experienced. They say hindsight is 20/20 but allow my story of video game addiction to be your **foresight**. When I tell you how addicted I was, it's not meant to scare you, it's meant to educate you and steer you away from making the mistakes I made and suffering the way I did.

When I looked back, I discovered that I didn't even realize what was happening to me. If you've read this far, I can only

became-the-most-addicting-game-in-history-5e827754f76a?gi=474010de8f3#:~:text=Children%20are%20becoming%20so%20addicted,heroin%2C%20according%20to%20some%20studies.

imagine what's happening to you is similar, and I want to help.

Chapter 5: A Toll on My Life

By the age of 15, video games had consumed my life. It had become my lifestyle, and people were starting to notice. It's embarrassing to look back now and realize all I cared about was video games while everyone around me was living their best lives. Video games had become my "friends". My peers were preparing to write college essays, socializing, and falling in and out of love.

At the time, I wasn't thinking about how I, too, could have all those things if I just put down the controller and quit gaming; I was in too deep.

My life became a monotonous routine of wake up, school, homework, volunteer, game, dinner, game, sleep (maybe), and repeat. I didn't even bother to do anything I didn't absolutely have to do. All I wanted and needed to do was game. At this point it didn't even matter what game I played; I just needed a controller in my hand. It felt like my life had become just me, a chair, and a screen with pixels–because that's exactly what it had become. It felt like that because *it was like that!* I never saw it coming, so I couldn't stop it from happening to me. There were no books like this one to help me see the light at the end of a very long tunnel while I was going through it. That's why I wrote one.

Remember what I said about hindsight? If I'd only known...

Around this time, I stopped participating in sports and avoided any social interaction that wasn't forced on me by my parents (and trust me, I found ways to get out of that to get back to my games too), because I truly prioritized my games and didn't think anything could be more important.

I know, I know, it sounds ridiculous now, right? How could video games be more important than family vacations or excelling at a sport? I agree with you! Video games were the worst decision I ever made, and if I could give my younger self advice, I would tell him "Tomer, unplug the console right now". Since I can't speak to my younger self, I'm speaking to you, and maybe your parents, and offering what I've learned so that you never have to wish you could talk your younger self out of making these choices.

I stopped interacting with my friends in the real world, furthering my isolation. However, I didn't believe I *was* isolated because I was lying to myself. I assumed that since I had online friends, they were just as good as having friends in the real world. I tried to forget about the real friends I had and focused even more on gaming.

At this point, video games had succeeded in completely disconnecting me from what was left of my reality. **It had gone too far, but I was too far gone to see it.**

My sleep was beginning to become compromised, and I was always exhausted (a physical toll on my body).

It shouldn't come as a surprise that most teenagers who game become night owls with reverse sleep schedules. This is detrimental to living a full life because school, sports, hobbies, and family time all take place during the day. Sleeping at least eight hours per night is vital for development during puberty. Without adequate sleep, the body and brain cannot function at an optimal level leading to vitamin deficiencies, migraines, and obesity. For me, it became a struggle to focus on school, and on a few occasions, I even found myself dozing off.

Lack of sleep is proven to cause hormone imbalances that result in mental health issues requiring psychological intervention. Eventually, I developed a heightened sense of anger and aggression; if someone criticized me or said anything I didn't agree with I would lash out and attack them verbally.

My addiction was beginning to take a toll on me that would affect the rest of my life.

Chapter 6: Family "Nuisance"

Looking back, when I was in the depths of my addiction, I realize that I didn't even take the time to spend time with my family. Nothing was *incentivized* for me. What could my family give me that my video games couldn't? I was using video games to create a false sense of happiness and security so that I didn't have to face the things that were causing me difficulty or frustration in my real life. The saddest part is that I truly believed I was happy. I'd given up everything for video games, and I still didn't see all the time, money, and life I was wasting on this fake world.

See, that's what addiction does to the brain: it creates a false sense of security.

Addiction says: "as long as you have what you're craving, you don't need anything else". This is just one of the many lies addiction tells you to keep you hooked. Addiction *literally rewires your brain* to think it *needs* whatever it is you've become addicted to. It doesn't have to be drugs or cigarettes. It can be something as seemingly innocuous as video games. These days, parents gift kids and teens iPads, Xboxes, and PS5's at such a young age that it becomes nearly impossible for them to escape the inevitable outcome of addiction. If parents stop gifting their kids and teens these items, there's a better chance of stopping addiction to screens before it starts.

Children of the world: don't shoot the messenger. I'm not here to ruin your life!

OK, back to me...

It got to the point I was running away from everyone just so I could get back to my computer and game my life away. I couldn't even enjoy a family vacation because all I could think about was what I was missing on my computer, with my games. Were new add-ons available? Did I miss a live stream? I know it sounds insane to people who have never been addicted to this kind of technology, but it's true: my brain was so deep into the addiction that I could've been in the middle of the ocean on a cruise and not notice the ocean all around me; I was consumed by the thought of being alone in my room with my consoles.

Even if you can't relate to my specific video game addiction, I know you can relate to the feeling of having to turn off your phone in certain situations and wondering what you're missing on the other side of the screen. Imagine how you feel turning your phone off in a movie theatre for a few hours; this is how I felt every second I was away from my games.

I'd become so addicted to my video games I couldn't even have fun anymore. My brain was so distracted by what I was missing behind the screen that nothing my parents offered me would snap me out of it. I needed to have my own "snap" moment, and it hadn't come yet.

Unfortunately, I ruined many other vacations and family events for myself because of my addiction. I had mentally checked out, even though I was physically present for all these things.

It wasn't even just the big things I was missing while still present physically; it was the small things most teens take for granted while living at home with their parents. Most teens come home with their faces buried in their phones and don't take the time to even acknowledge their parents or siblings. "How was your day?" is met with grunts and groans. Parents or siblings try to engage in conversation and are met with a phone screen in their face, leaving them feeling ignored and unappreciated. Remember: you only get one set of parents. If you're lucky, they're attentive and present in your life, giving you a strong upbringing with good morals and education the way my parents have for my sister and me. Squandering the time, patience, and attention your parents give you is wasting a blessing you won't have forever.

My parents do everything to give me the best life possible, and back then I was throwing it in their face. I'd like to say it was the video games that were causing me to do a complete 180-degree personality shift, but I'd become an addict, and it was my responsibility to find a way out of that addiction and become a better person because of it.

I was learning lessons the hard way, but you don't have to!

That's why I wrote this book. Having gained knowledge and insight from my own addiction, I feel it's now my responsibility to help other children, teenagers, as well as their parents understand the signs of addiction. Sometimes you could be looking right at it and it's not clear what you're dealing with. It took more than seven precious years of my life to recognize these signs, and it's important for me to share them with you.

Months before my 16th birthday, my addiction ramped up to not just *playing* video games but to buying virtual products like skins and add-ons that I thought would contribute something significant to my life. Let me tell you, these game packs aren't cheap.

I was spending hundreds if not thousands of dollars of my allowance on non-tangible garbage. I couldn't hold or touch these products: my virtual character was using virtual trash that I spent real money for. If you don't already know, I'll make it crystal clear: buying in-game content is useless. Where does it go when you turn off the game? What will you do with it when you finish the game? It goes nowhere and you won't do one thing with it. It's, again, the metaphor of flushing money down the toilet. I think back now on all the things I could've used my allowance on, and I'm ashamed and embarrassed that I wasted it on in-game content. This is another way that video game developers get players hooked. "Forcing" players to purchase in-game content to proceed to a new level or to "unlock" different areas of the game that can't be accessed without in-app purchases.

I get it, businesses need money, but doing it at the expense of impressionable children and teenagers is immoral and lacks the necessary regulations to prevent addiction. Unfortunately, even if game developers gave away the extra content, it wouldn't be any less addictive. Every time a game releases new content, it's a reward for the player. Dopamine is created through the process of stimulating the striatum, or the reward center of the brain. On MRI scans of addicts, this "pleasure center" of the brain is lit up.

On a person without any form of addiction, the striatum is dormant until the person engages in an activity that brings them joy.[6] It's true, Google it!

Video games had become my only source of happiness. They controlled my thoughts, and I found them to be the only worthwhile activity in my day. My world now consisted of school (because I had to go, to avoid jail and all that) and my room with my games. School, sports, family,

---

[6] Kühn, S., Romanowski, A., Schilling, C., Lorenz, R., Mörsen, C., Seiferth, N., Banaschewski, T., Barbot, A., Barker, G. J., Büchel, C., Conrod, P. J., Dalley, J. W., Flor, H., Garavan, H., Ittermann, B., Mann, K., Martinot, J.-L., Paus, T., Rietschel, M., … Gallinat, J. (2011, November 15). *The neural basis of video gaming*. Translational psychiatry. Retrieved June 2, 2022, from https://www.ncbi.nlm.nih.gov/pmc/articles/PMC3309473/

and friends all became roadblocks to the one thing I really wanted: video games. I'd become a lousy person to be around because when I wasn't daydreaming of my games, I was complaining that I couldn't play them. Who wants to spend time with someone who constantly complains or doesn't even want to be there? I could've been a meme, and not a very funny one. Trust me when I tell you, you don't want to be a meme.

What I did become was the one thing my parents instilled in my sister and me never to be: a quitter. Though, looking back now I feel that if I'd quit video games sooner, they'd have been fine with 'quitter' applied to that.

My life only got worse from there. Even video games stopped giving me 'good feelings' unless I played for 12+ hours a day. I used to be able to play for an hour and feel the excitement of the game; years into becoming a "gamer", I found myself no longer able to achieve this sort of excitement. Yet, I still played and played, chasing that next game high, hoping to feel the way I once did about gaming.

I could remember the feeling of receiving my first Xbox console, but I couldn't achieve the high anymore. I was becoming numb to everyone and everything around me. I was trapped in a mindset of constant apathy and boredom. Nothing was fun, nothing was meaningful, and I was stuck in an endless loop of video game hell. It was only a matter of time before "the snap" occurred, but I wasn't aware of it yet. The mindset I found myself in, one of pure apathy for everything, created a scary situation for my parents. They weren't sure how to proceed in doing what was best for me versus what would make me happy.

In my home, my parents set a careful and well thought out balance of giving my sister and me what we wanted while maintaining rules and boundaries for us. We always had what we needed so long as all that was required of us was accomplished.

At the time, I didn't have the adequate decision-making skills to know that video games would hook me, and that I would eventually become addicted to them. I can laugh about it with my family now, but deep into my addiction, my parents were scared for my life and future. If I didn't have "the snap" soon, they were going to have to enact tough love whether I liked it or not. I can proudly say my parents raised a smart teen and I'm becoming an even smarter young adult. My mom and dad never had to enact tough love, because what happened next is a testament to how I was raised to understand right and wrong, even in the depths of my addiction.

As I've stated before, addiction stops you from progressing in life. That constant dopamine chase hurts you more than it helps you. Constantly chasing something you'll never reach disconnects you from reality and hurts the ones around you. It *is* possible to stop, though, if you truly want to. If you want your life back enough, you can reach out and grab it; there is a light at the end of a very dark tunnel. I like to call this light, "the snap".

Chapter 7: "The Snap"

Every addict has a moment known colloquially as "rock bottom".

Picture this: my 17th birthday is coming up, and I'm driving home from school. As I'm driving home, I get the sudden feeling that I'm missing something; phone, backpack, wallet–all there. I took a mental inventory of what was missing, and all my things were in the car with me. What I was missing wasn't a material object, but I didn't understand it in the moment. As I continued driving home, something dawned on me: I was missing time.

It was like in cartoons, when a lightbulb appears above a character's head when they have an idea. Suddenly, I felt as if I'd been abducted by a UFO for years and had just been returned to planet Earth. I felt out of body until that moment in the car, but I didn't know why. I couldn't explain why I suddenly felt like myself again so suddenly, when for years prior I didn't even know "I" had been gone. I was Tomer again! Where had he disappeared to, though? And that's the moment I knew...

Tomer Shaked had disappeared behind a screen, chained to his video game controller. He was back now, and he had a lot of work to do.

I was in a state of shock, trying my best to focus on the road while my head began to spin. I asked myself, "was I even me?". I knew the answer to that. Of course, I wasn't me. I'd been so lost in a fake, video game world for so many years that I'd completely lost my identity. I felt like I'd become a video game character, not a real person. I was flooded with so many emotions I couldn't make sense of them all at once, and I started to cry. That was IT: the moment I decided to never touch another video game again. I wasn't going to "cut back" on gaming time. I wasn't going to "play less". I was Done with a capital D.

There wasn't a single second I considered how hard it would be to **stop cold turkey**. All the energy and effort and wasted time I poured into video games was about to be used as a sort of self-motivation to kick video games right then and there. I was so determined to shut it down forever. I had a new goal: I wanted to do something great with my life. I would spend my time away from the screen, figuring out what I wanted to do and who I wanted to become.

Many kids and teenagers who I've seen quit video games share a similar situation to my own. Most of us felt the deep sorrow of missing out so much *life* because of video games. The second I got home, I started to make the changes that would move my life forward, and I wasn't spending a single second looking back.

Chapter 8: Radical Change

I was a man on a mission. I didn't talk to anyone, I just kept moving through the house and directly to where I kept my games. I marched straight to my consoles and computer, and it was like I was programmed to get this done. I deleted my accounts, my progress, and all the applications associated with my gaming. I never thought this would be something I could do, but there I was, taking my life back into my own hands by quitting video gaming cold turkey. I couldn't even believe it was happening in the moment, but I would have time to reflect later. In that moment, the games needed to go.

I piled up all my gaming equipment and put it away. That was it. I was done with it. No more Discord, no more Xbox, no more wasted life. I never looked back and since then, I've never had the desire to play again. It took a long time, more than seven years, but I was crystal clear on having a future that did not include video games. I wanted to get to know people again, including myself. I needed time to figure out who Tomer was, and what kind of person I could be. There were so many things I'd be able to achieve now that video games were out of my life forever. I was no longer moving backwards in life. It was time to go full steam ahead with the brilliant future my parents had always seen for me, a future I could now see, too!

I began to process what I had done, and I asked myself the question, "how will you spend all your newfound time?" I didn't know the answer to that question just then.

The only thing I knew at that moment was that my life was about to change forever–for the better. I had gifted *myself* a second chance to make things right. I did not intend to waste a second of making up for lost time. Knowing I couldn't really get the time back, the only thing I could do was look forward and pursue a better future for myself. I never looked back at my gaming life. Mary Engelbreit once said: "Don't look back, you're not going that way". This quote describes exactly what I planned to do with my new life.

This new and improved life included more focus on academics, extra-curricular activities, and a sport that I love: rowing.

Since quitting gaming, the way I've made up for lost time has shocked my parents, teachers, and coaches. I try to stay humble, work hard, and never brag about my achievements but I will tell you, I feel like a brand new Tomer. I'm better than I've ever been, and so proud of myself. My accomplishments since "the snap", I've been told, have been remarkable.

I want to share some of my accomplishments with you, so that you understand what is possible once you cut the cord on gaming and plug into your life.

Since cutting the cord I have:

- Returned to rowing, receiving a varsity award

- Joined the school Spanish competition team and competed in state competition where I receive first prize. I also received the school's Spanish Language Scholar Award.

- Completed a law fellowship for high school juniors

- Attended a leadership seminar

- Joined a beach cleanup crew

- Volunteered with the Jack & Jill Center

A note on the Jack & Jill Center: The Center provides indigent children a place to spend their days under the care of loving adults who provide academic learning and social skills. The Jack & Jill Center is a place dear to my heart, and I want to take a moment to explain to you the impact it made on my life.

The Center is rich in history. The Jack & Jill Center was established in 1942 courtesy of the Junior League of Greater Fort Lauderdale. It served and continues to serve as an emergency nursery school, providing childcare; first, during World War II to women entering the workforce. Now, it's a haven for impoverished families who want the best for their children. The Jack & Jill Center provides childcare in a safe, happy environment for underprivileged children who may have otherwise been deprived the ability to learn and grow safely.

More specifically, Jack & Jill describes its extensive services as: "a nonprofit 501(c)(3) community-based organization that provides comprehensive, holistic, wraparound support services to children of high-need parents who work or attend school in order to improve their wellbeing and quality of life."

None of these accomplishments would have been possible if I was still gaming 12+ hours a day. Cutting the cord has opened my eyes to how many people in my community are in need and has freed my time and energy to be able to help people.

After quitting video games, I learned to use my time more wisely. I amassed hundreds of volunteer hours and will soon reach a milestone of over 400 of community service hours. Volunteering my time has changed my life in remarkable ways.

I have so much more I want to do, and I wake up every day with the ability to make all my dreams and goals a reality. I even have time for fun hobbies that never crossed my mind while I was gaming. I am back to playing piano and guitar, and I recently taught myself to write with my left hand! Now, I'm officially an ambidextrous musician.

You think this happened overnight? Not exactly. To really understand how I achieved this level of success and fulfillment, we've got to throw it back to "the before". Before the radical change, before the new Tomer appeared.

It's time to talk about the night of "the snap".

There was a lot of work to be done before I could call any of the accomplishments I talked about my own.

Chapter 9: The Sacrifice

The first night, I spent hours fixing up the space where my games were once hooked up. I had to make sure everything was gone, and not a trace of it remained to lure me back in. The problem with addiction is, even if you quit cold turkey, there's always a temptation to go back to it if it's there. I knew if I saw my games around, I might want to play again, no matter how much I'd convinced myself that I was done.

After all, you know what they say about good intentions.

I made sure my parents knew to never give the games back. I specifically told them: "mom, dad, take them and put them somewhere I never have to see them again." My parents were shocked, but they were by my side the entire night, helping me eliminate every trace of gaming in our home.

In the following chapters, when I talk about my achievements after I quit video games, I want to be transparent and honest about how I lifted myself out of gaming addiction and the time and hard work I put into getting there. As they say, "Rome wasn't built in a day". I didn't quit video games and immediately achieve my goals. There was a learning curve, a time where I needed to challenge myself to not only stay away from video games forever, but to do something valuable with my time and energy. It wasn't enough to quit the video games. I needed to make moves, big ones, ones that would improve my life and help me in my future. I started small: a walk on the beach, calling a friend, and learning to write with my left hand. Small steps are still important steps.

Building on my small steps, I was able to achieve what some people thought was impossible. Without video games in my life, I realized *nothing* was impossible for me. In the beginning stages of kicking any addiction, you need someone (in this case: parents) to hold you accountable. This was a lonely time in my life. I had just erased every trace of video games from my life. I deleted all my progress, which took years to achieve, and canceled all my subscriptions. I was giving myself a fresh start, but I won't deny it, at first I was empty without video games. I hadn't yet discovered ways to fill my time productively; it'd been years since I wanted to do anything except play games with my free time. However, in time, I would see how beautiful the world could be, and how fulfilling life could become once I cut the cord forever. That's why, If I wanted to play, or started to talk about video games, my parents were going to get tough–and get tough fast. Any conversation about gaming was going to be shut down and corrected before I could fall back into addictive habits.

My parents are loving people, but I personally asked them to get tough and lay down the law if I ever considered touching a video game again.

As I was cleaning up my former gaming area, I began to take stock of just how much time I wasted. It was time I could never, ever get back, and it motivated me to keep going, keep cleaning up the space and ridding it of every trace that video games had ever been there. Cords, cables, controllers: all gone. As I cleaned and organized, I had epiphany after epiphany.

As I mentioned previously, money loss was another consequence of my addiction. I spent so much money, ridiculous amounts of money, on games. Sometimes I never even played the games I bought because I had so many. I spent money on items and equipment that I wouldn't use or used once and never gave another look. Gaming caused me to spend a fortune on things that didn't contribute to any significant sense of my well-being. All it did for me was eat up my time and drain my allowance.

The last and possibly most significant sacrifice I endured through my addiction to video games was the loss of the excitement and happiness that the hobby of gaming once gave me. When I stopped gaming, I didn't understand anything about dopamine or what, exactly, had happened to my brain. All I knew was that video games had eaten up years of my life, drained my limited allowance, and in hindsight, it made me miserable. I had no idea there was so much science behind what was going on inside my brain.

Something I learned from cutting the console cord is that it's essential to be truthful with yourself. My parents instilled in me to never lie to *others*, and that's important. However, through my addiction I learned that I couldn't lie to *myself*. So, don't lie to yourself and be completely honest with yourself. Take stock of what's going on inside your brain, because only you can truly know what's happening in your innermost thoughts. No one can read your mind. Only you can know if something is right or wrong for you.

You may be doing something you shouldn't: staying up late, hanging out with the wrong group of friends, or doing something that will hurt you more than it will help you. If this sounds like your life: Stop. Change course before you're too far down the wrong path to come back. For many who are older and reading my story, you may not have someone in your life that will push you into making such a radical change, if that's the case, you'll have to hold yourself accountable.

You can't rely on other people to make decisions about the course of your life. If something feels wrong, don't do it. You have the power to choose. Don't wait for your parents, siblings, or friends to tell you what you should be doing; that's how so many of us get into the mess that is addiction in the first place. We wait for someone to point out what we're doing is wrong instead of being truthful with ourselves. We develop adaptive responses to criticism about our behavior and blame others for our flaws.

Have your own back so you can kick your own addiction.

Chapter 10: What to Expect After Quitting

Now that you've hopefully made the decision to quit, I want to explore what comes next.

Consider the pages of this book a friend that wants you to do what's best for you. I'll leave some blank pages in the back of this book that you can use to write down your own thoughts on kicking your gaming addiction. You don't have to share them with anyone but writing down what it feels like to break free of gaming can be helpful. It was for me. You'll go through every emotion imaginable and reading your feelings back weeks or months later will help you understand just how far you've come.

Gaming consumed nearly every free waking hour of my days, for years. It took over every second I was awake and free to do what I wanted.

After I quit, I began to fall in love with so many hobbies and activities again. As my brain began to recover its dopamine through intense self-talk, focus, and the cold turkey approach to quitting, I began to feel joyful emotions again. The brain can recover its ability to feel happiness with time if you stay away from the games and don't slip back into addictive habits. Things made me happy! I felt satisfied when I completed a task my parents asked me to do.

I filled my days with academics, sports, and friends. I fell right back into old friendships I thought were gone forever. Without a gaming addiction, my friends accepted me back into their lives and I discovered that we still had so much in common!

I couldn't believe how big and incredible the world had become while I'd been "away"! I had no idea what achievements and true happiness was waiting just around the corner!

After I quit gaming, part of the joy I felt was experiencing everything life had to offer. These were things I never thought I could enjoy again. I was spending time with my family and friends. I started exercising my body to regain the health I'd lost both physically and mentally over the course of seven plus years of addiction.

My story has a happy ending, and because we took this rollercoaster ride of addiction together throughout the book, I want to share some of the benefits you can expect from quitting video games:

More Time: When you ditch the games, the world will open back up to you. You'll find yourself enjoying more free time throughout the day. You'll notice that there are so many things available to elevate your life to another level. Greatness will become yours for the taking. The only thing holding you back from being great and living your best life was video games. Now that you've dropped those bad habits, everything is possible.

Time is a commodity **you will never get more of, so use it wisely and for the best.**

Fewer Distractions: Gaming keeps you from engaging in the things you *need* to do such as chores, homework, your job, preparing for college, etc. They also keep you from things you *want* to do such as playing a sport, spending time with friends and family, learning a new hobby like cooking or art, exercising, or other forms of self-care. Cutting video games out of your life dramatically reduces the distractions in your life and it frees you up to live fully. Through ditching the games, you'll become focused on what is essential.

You'll prioritize whatever you're working toward in your life. When you quit video games, you'll be able to plan for a future. For the teens reading this: spending your life wasting away in front of a screen is *so cringe.*

Reconnect to Reality: Without the distraction of video games, you'll be able to repair and rekindle relationships with your family and your friends. Now, I'm not saying it'll be easy, but it can be done. The people in your life who care about you will understand that you're working through an addiction and do their best to have your back while you return to the real world. You'll be able to socialize again, and you'll be much more open to conversation and putting yourself out there to meet new people and try new things.

The real world is an adventure that's waiting for you to explore it, don't miss out on it!

Personal Development: With more time and fewer distractions, you can work on things that will increase your value as a person. You may be preparing for college in the next couple years and may have wasted a lot of time that could've been spent visiting and researching universities as well as building an academic future, on video games.

It's never too late to rebuild.

Talk to your teachers about extra credit assignments, AP and honors courses, and dual enrollment opportunities that can get you back on track. Get involved in the community and join outreach programs that can help your city and help you socialize again. If you're honest about wanting to rebuild academically, I can promise you that your teachers and academic counselors will want to help you get there.

Video games may have taken a toll on your physical health, too. Focus on finding ways to move your body that feels good. Go for a walk with a friend, find a new sport you like to play, or join an in-person or virtual gym. Take small steps to regain any physical health you might have lost from gaming. You may be feeling sloppy or unfit after years behind a screen. Video games take things like academics, personal style, and physical health away from you, but you can take them back.

Open To More Opportunities: While in the throes of a gaming addiction, you may have lost sight of short- and long-term goals you once set for yourself. Gaming is a time suck, and by moving those resources elsewhere, you can increase your chances of long-term success and happiness. Do a favor for a friend to show you care, complete your chores on time for your parents, study an extra 20 minutes, learn a new language, or volunteer. Without video games stealing your time, you'll be able to engage in opportunities that can provide a better future for yourself, and leave your mark on the community you live in.

More Time with Family and Friends: People are what make life special, not video games. If you were to list the five most important things in life, the universal #1 is Family. Only addicts would list the things that are ultimately hurting them at the top of their list. What will you choose? The memories you will make with your family and friends are essential and shouldn't be cast aside for screen time. You don't want to live with the regret that you could have spent more time with someone, making memories that last.

I personally experienced these benefits and more after I quit gaming for good. I have elevated my life to something greater than it ever was before. My mom says my life "took off like a shooting star" once the games were gone. Yours can too. It's hard to see if you haven't begun the process of kicking the habit, but if you've read this far, I know for a fact that your "shooting star" is on the way, too.

You'll understand once you quit, that it's the best thing you've ever done for yourself.

These photos are my story... now go create your own!

Chapter 11: Why Should I Quit?

There's a profound change that happens to you when you quit video games, and it's what will ultimately keep you from ever touching a video game again. The profound change happens when you understand what's important in life. As I said previously, it's important to never look back.

Quitting video games was one of the best choices I ever made for myself and my family. It gave my life meaning again. It made me want to get up every day to discover new things and experience the world. When I was gaming, I wasn't present at all. I was *physically* present, yes, but otherwise I was doing nothing to better myself. Quitting gave me back a sense of curiosity, of discovering that I love to learn new things. Moving my body through sports and exercise helped me cope with my new reality.

But why should you quit video games? Sometimes, what makes us happy isn't necessarily what's best for us. Gaming is one of those things that makes you happy in the moment but can hurt you in the long run. Every day is something precious, and we can't waste it isolating ourselves from the real world, no matter how tough life gets. If we resort to the screen over interacting with people and expressing our feelings effectively during times of stress, anxiety, pain, and boredom, it ultimately prevents us from becoming who we're meant to be; whole, well-rounded human beings with futures so unbelievably great it's hard to put into words.

Through the journey of writing this book, I reflected on all the things I missed out on at a young age because of gaming. What could I have done with all that time I wasted? Sometimes taking the first step to a future you can't yet see is difficult. You may find that distracting yourself from planning a great future is easier than taking the first step. For me, and many of you reading this, that distraction, that isolating thing is video games.

The power to change for the better will be challenging, and maybe it's still difficult for you to maintain the ability to stay away from games complete, but I promise you that your future self will thank you.

Save yourself from the same regret I feel now and quit because you've got to do something extraordinary to get to where you want to be. And yes, that extraordinary thing you should do today is **quit**. Sometimes you must sacrifice something fun, for something worthwhile.

There's an old saying: "all things worth having require sacrifice worth giving". That says it all. For you to achieve greatness in your life, you must take drastic steps and sacrifice one unhealthy habit to better every other aspect of your life.

Your family, your friends, and even your peers at school can help you quit. You are not alone and should never feel ashamed asking for help from a parent, teacher, counselor, or friend.

I hope by reading my story you feel a sense of friendship from me, an outstretched hand here to help pull you out of the deep end of your gaming addiction.

Afterword

First, I want to thank you, reader, for taking the time to read this diary of my journey to cutting the console cord. This book tells the story of the last seven years of my life and how addiction could've destroyed me, but instead I chose to learn and grow into the person I am today. I wrote this book to inspire people to take control of their lives and quit gaming for good.

Life is so important, and unlike in games, we only live once–or so I'm told.

There are no repeats on this journey, no refunds on the time we waste, no recreating memories that we lose when we choose to sit in front of a screen instead of joining the world and the human experience. You must make a choice of how to spend your time: will it be in front of a screen or in front of people?

Throughout those gaming years, my parents used to ask me every weekend to go with them to the beach, to the movies, and to dinners. I always said no and went back to gaming. After I quit, I decided to join them one Saturday, and what I discovered changed my perspective on life. There was still a chair at the dinner table for me, and my family still wanted to spend quality time on the beach with me. They hadn't given up on me, and it made me even more aware that I should never give up on myself.

I hope this book helps you take control of your life and quit gaming for good. I hope this book has given you a different perspective on how you view video gaming. My hope is that by reading this book, you can understand the harm video games are causing you.

Remember: I've been where you are right now. Quitting your video game addiction is the hardest thing you'll ever do, but you can do it, and I wish you the best of luck on your journey.

This book was not written for financial gain, as I believe it would detract from my journey and my intentions of helping other kids and teens overcome their video game addictions. After much consideration I've decided that 100% of

the proceeds will be donated to the *Jack &*
Jill Center.

The Parental Perspective

Reading Tomer's book brought an ocean of emotions to the surface. As my husband and I read each word, we began to question our parenting abilities and asked ourselves questions: "Where did we go wrong?" "Why Tomer?" "What caused the addiction and what more could we have done as his parents to have prevented it?"

These questions and second-guesses caused many sleepless nights.

In the earlier years when Tomer was first introduced to video games, it was done in an open space, in our home. Usually, it involved his friends who came over to join the fun. It was social, and it was harmless, because it wasn't excessive; it was a source of entertainment. Little did we know that this leisure activity would consume Tomer completely. If we had known that video game addiction could change a child's entire personality and cause behavioral issues, we would have immediately put a stop to it.

As parents, we wanted only for Tomer's happiness, health, and safety. When so many children Tomer's age were playing video games, we didn't believe we had anything to worry about. Of course, we were the strict parents; nothing got past us or so we believed. If something "sketchy" as the kids say, was going on in our home, we knew about it.

However, we never denied our children the ability to have fun in a safer manner once homework and extracurriculars were attended to. Our children are everything to my husband and me. When they cry, we cry; when they're happy, we're happy. When they achieve something incredible, we could not be prouder of them. That's why reading Tomer's book hit us so hard; being unable to see how miserable our son was, made us feel miserable, too. Most parents will tell you they don't understand their teens, but this was something much worse for us.

It's one thing to not understand the memes and language teens are using in 2022, but to not understand the deep isolation and misery your child is going through, as parents who have always been present and available to them, was crushing.

Had we known video game addiction was silently prevalent among kids his age, we would've jumped into action. If he played video games at a friend's house, we couldn't have stopped him, but we wouldn't have allowed him to continue to play in our home, even for leisure.

All of this is not to say that all he did is play video games. That is not the case. His school schedule involved two hours on the road each day, as well as seven hours at school. There was not much time for "fun" if you also take into consideration the hours he spent on homework, sporting activities, and volunteering at various organizations. However, aside from these *mandatory* demands on his time (emphasis on "mandatory"), every free minute he did have was spent playing video games and that included summers and school breaks.

At first, we said to ourselves "well, he is doing good in school, and he is playing with friends at home or online, so he is socializing and having fun at the same time." We wanted him to feel rested and happy. We thought he would get better grades and excel in his extracurricular requirements if he was able to rest and socialize with friends.

Unfortunately, as the years went by, entertainment for our son turned into a nightmare for our family. We watched as Tomer invited friends to our home less and less. It was as if we were watching our son disappear into an alternate reality of video games. He hated traveling (something we enjoy doing as a family) and each time he agreed to travel with us, it was only after an argument where he was *forced* to go. Extended family dinners became time away from his games, a distraction, and we were beginning to feel he didn't even want to sit at the table and eat a meal with us.

As parents, we knew that Tomer was spending too much time playing video games. Parents know their own child better than anyone, but it was the severity of his condition that we did not understand. The not wanting to travel and avoiding family dinners weren't the first clues for us, but they solidified what we already knew about our son. In our hearts we were certain Tomer was gaming too much, that it was the reason for his complete change in personality, but we struggled with the war inside us: video games made our son happy, but was that what was best for his health and future at the time?

At one point, Tomer was becoming a highly skilled and recognized gamer (he had a popular YouTube channel with lots of followers who subscribed to his channel to watch him play video games) and we did our best to convince ourselves that we should be supportive of him. If this was in fact his passion, we should encourage him to do what he loves.

Many parents struggle with this same doubt. Parents may see other children gaming and because it's such a popular pastime for teens, they figure there's nothing to worry about.

We always had our own dreams for Tomer, but at some point, we thought that "if he's good at this, we won't stop him". As we continued to try and rationalize what was happening, our reaction seemed to change weekly, if not daily.

One week we would get so upset we'd argue with him endlessly, ultimately forcing him to spend time with us. The next week my husband and I would fight amongst ourselves over his gaming habits, where one of us would yell at the other to yell at our son. My husband and I are lawyers, formally trained in effective communication skills in both the office and the court room. We understand how to act reasonably to solve time sensitive problems.

Our son's gaming addiction was uncharted territory for us. It was causing us to fight in a way we never had before. We were so filled with sadness and anger that when we tried to have an effective conversation, it always ended with one of us raising our voice.

Tomer is an extremely respectful and obedient child (this is one thing that never changed) so when we told him to take breaks, he respected our decision and took breaks. Seeing the sadness on his face when we asked him to stop gaming hurt us more than his time playing video games. So eventually, we allowed him to get back to it, only wanting him to be happy.

We only had one condition if he was going to continue to game at the level he'd reached: he must keep up his good grades. In our home, Bs were not acceptable, and we made sure Tomer understood this.

As you know from reading the pages before this, Tomer quit video games entirely on his own. He wanted more from life all on his own, and he achieved that. It was his own epiphany, his "snap", that brought on the change in him. But this is not to say that as parents we should give up and let it happen on its own. We must try, and if we're able to, we should seek professional help when it's appropriate to do so.

We hope that parents reading our son's story understand that we were lost ourselves and felt like we failed him. We were lucky that our son quit on his own, as we honestly don't know what we would've done if he couldn't do so. For us, we were unprepared to seek a deeper level of help with Tomer's video game addiction. We don't feel it's our place to offer advice on any form of psychiatric help within this book. We're not doctors, we're just loving parents to our son.

As my husband and I were contemplating what to do, watching the clock of life ticking day in and day out, we thought of ideas that we wanted to implement, before Tomer quit gaming.

We were aware that kids and teens respond well to a reward system (a much healthier version of the reward system for the brain, provided by video games). What felt best for us was trying to come up with list of goals for Tomer and assigned a reward for each completed goal.

Knowing that not all kids and teens can quit gaming cold turkey, it might help if parents create lists of goals (things to do) so that their child will be able to focus on getting these things done and use video gaming only as a reward. By focusing on what needs to get done and achieving goals, the child may not even realize that they are playing less and less.

We cannot expect everyone to quit gaming overnight and that's OK.

It's only important to see progress made. This progress should be in the form of the child or teen stepping away from gaming a little bit more each day.

Every day is a new day filled with hopes, dreams, and goals to achieve. If everyday a child plays even half an hour less, in time, it adds up to hours otherwise wasted playing video games. Many teens fall in love with volunteering or teaching themselves new skills. Once these ideas are presented to them, video games may not be as "bright and shiny" as they once were.

For Tomer, beach cleanups and rowing have become his passions. Showing kids and teens what the world has to offer as if it's a reward can be helpful in removing them from in front of the   screen.

Like any challenge in life, so long as the parents see the progress, you should celebrate it. Being a parent is the most difficult job there is, so celebrate the small victories and consider yourself successful. Regardless of how long it may take, so long as today is better than yesterday, you are doing alright.

As parents, our children's happiness is everything to us. Finding out that our child's happiness had been narrowly reduced to video games felt like an avalanche tumbling down on our family. We did not know how to stop it and we lashed out, communicating ineffectively many times.

Through writing his book, Tomer understood the consequences of ineffective communication. He knows now how video game addiction can cause a breakdown in being able to socialize with others. We won't lie to you, as parents this was a lesson learned for us as well. You can always learn from your children.

Over the course of many years, we saw how with each day that went by,

Tomer's interest in family, friends, or anything outside of his gaming circle was diminishing to the point that even coming to his "home office" (where he did most of his gaming and YouTube'ing) to say 'hi' in the afternoon felt like we were just a bother to him. He did not even acknowledge we were home. We always had the sinking feeling that we were bothering him, that he didn't want us around.

At a certain point, we became so resentful of being dismissed that we stopped asking him to join us.

Let's be real: we knew it was wrong to stop inviting our own son to join us, but it was how we coped with the situation. We love our son, and our daughter loves her brother, and we wanted him in our lives, making memories with us. To deal with the rejection and sadness the three of us were feeling, we told ourselves that he will grow out of gaming 'eventually', and that if Tomer was happy, we were happy.

We did believe however, that "eventually" was happening any time soon. So, what happened shortly after that, shocked us when, out of the blue Tomer announced that he was no longer playing any video game, ever again. When we learned that he'd made the choice to delete all his accounts, lose all his progress, and close his YouTube channel, we panicked. We knew that once he deleted it all, there was no going back to the way things were. We had no playbook, so to speak, for this kind of change in our son, and weren't sure what to expect from the 'withdrawal' process of video game addiction.

For Tomer, there was no 'withdrawal'; he simply never looked back at his gaming life and that was that. We never heard another word about video games in our house again, until he told us he wrote this book about his experience.

We can vividly remember yelling at him (in our shocked state of mind) for closing all his accounts, deleting his progress, and 'quitting' or 'giving up'. The change in our son was so quick and happened so smoothly, that for a moment we forgot that this is what we'd been praying for, and that it was happening.

It was all Tomer. He decided to quit. In a single second, driving home from school, he decided he was done with video games and wanted his life back. We didn't understand why. He just told us that he "missed so much of his life and that people and family are the most important in life".

We were happy, of course, we'd prayed for this moment for years, but we were also scared because we had no idea if at any moment, he'd regret his decision.

Tomer's transformation was an overnight event. Nothing has been the same since.

Ironically, it took my husband and me months to process something that took our son only minutes, seconds even. We spent many sleepless nights talking about the dramatic and positive transformation that was taking place in front of our eyes every day. We felt we could breathe again.

We take no credit for it and if anything, we regret the way in which we reacted initially. We were not as supportive as we could've been at first because we were shocked and worried that the change we were witnessing wasn't real. We believed in our son; we just couldn't process the change as quickly as he decided to make it happen.

We don't have any family members or friends that had to deal with addiction, and especially not to the point that it caused problems in their lives. Life after

Tomer kicked video games was as uncharted for us as the addiction.

As we were going through processing the before-and-after and what our family had experienced, we only then realized that Tomer was officially addicted to video games. His "snap," as he refers to it, was the "antidote" to the "poison" that was video games.

Tomer is driven, determined, happy, active, healthy, and an extremely social teen. We give him all the credit because the change came from within him; his mind and heart were ready to quit, and he listened to his instincts.

Still, reading this book it hurts our hearts just as much as we felt the pain of living through it. We did not know that it was an addiction. We had no idea that such an addiction existed. It's not easy for parents to see it coming. We want you to know if you missed the signs, it's not your fault.

Tomer was strong enough to realize that he had a problem on his own, without our help. He realized that he needed to change, and he understood that the change must be drastic. He never looked back at his decision, and with the way he's filled his life with advanced classes in school, rowing, and volunteering, he does not have the time to look back and dwell on the past.

It saddens him at times, when he thinks about the moments, what he lost to video games. He knows that he cannot get those moments back, and the realization of what was lost forever has made him cry more than once. It makes him sad to know that there are so many teens who are in the same situation he was in not long ago. These teens may not know how to get out of it. The way Tomer explains his "snap" in the book is meant to help those teens who want out of video gaming life and can't get there. Tomer wants to be their helping hand through this text.

His goal is to change their lives for the better. With teens, there is a struggle to get through to them because like Tomer *was*, they are so deep into the addiction that they don't understand what is happening to them and how it's affecting their families and future.

We feel blessed that Tomer was able to understand the severity of his addiction to video games and the negative affect it had on all aspects of his life, mostly family. We hope that other parents who realize their children are in the dark, dark world of gaming addiction will be able to do more, earlier on in their children's lives so that they will not look back at lost time and carry this pain in their heart.

There is another way—through this book. With video game addiction, tough love will need to be implemented if children cannot be strong enough to stop this addiction on their own, the way Tomer was able to.

Game Over: **Bonus Content**

QUIZ: Are You Addicted to Gaming? (No cheating!)

Answer all questions honestly to find out if video games may be a problem in your life.

Do you spend more than 1-2 hours a day in front of a screen play video games?

[ ] Yes [ ] No

How many hours per day do you spend playing video games/on social media?

[ ] 1-2 [ ] 3-5 [ ] I don't even want to count

Has your homework, friendships, and/or family life changed after you started playing video games?

[ ] Yes [ ] No

Do you find yourself spending more time in your room than with family and friends?

[ ] Yes [ ] No

When was the last time you socialized, volunteered, or spent time with people you care about (excluding socializing in school)?

[ ] Today [ ] Yesterday [ ] Last week [ ] I can't even remember because it's been so long...

Have your parents or friends asked you to join them for an activity you didn't want to do because you'd rather be playing video games?

[ ] Yes [ ] No

Have your parents asked you to stop playing video games and/or restricted how much time you're allowed to play games?

[ ] Yes [ ] No

If you answered "NO" 3 out of 7 of these questions, you may want to talk to a family member, teacher, or friend about how much time you're spending on gaming.

This is a tool to help understand how video games may be affecting your life, not medical advice. This quiz was created by a former game addict to help teens who may find themselves struggling with gaming addiction.

GAME OVER: FREE WRITING JOURNAL

USE THESE FREE WRITING PAGES TO
JOURNAL YOUR THOUGHTS ON HOW
GAMING HAS AFFECTED YOUR LIFE.

GAME OVER: FREE WRITING JOURNAL

GAME OVER: FREE WRITING JOURNAL

GAME OVER: FREE WRITING JOURNAL

Acknowledgements

First: Big thanks to those who made *Game Over* possible.

I would like to take a moment to thank all those who supported me throughout this process; those who provided encouraging words and those who gave constructive criticism, even when I did not enjoy it very much.

First, I would like to thank my parents who supported me in my journey of writing this book. You gave me the push and support I needed and created an environment in which I can grow and succeed. I could not have done it without you.

I would also like to thank Molly Schlom, my editor, who worked tirelessly to help me figure out the intricate aspects of writing a book: from obtaining ISBN, to selecting a publishing company. Thank you, also, for guiding me on copyright to protect my hard work.

I did not realize how much work is required from putting my thoughts into printed words, to the final product: holding the book in my hands. You helped me brainstorm for hours on what would be the best title for the book and who should be commissioned to design the cover, using my specific ideas and colors. I must have changed the book title 9 times and for each name selected, you always gave constructive input. You taught me to focus on the reader and what the title and cover design will mean to them.

Big thank you to Amanda Martini-Hughes, who reviewed my final product during the review process and helped me clarify what I was attempting to convey. You taught me how to organize my thoughts on paper. Your insight throughout the process was tremendous, and I have learned so much through your kind, constructive criticism.

Made in the USA
Las Vegas, NV
18 August 2022

53522330R00095